Happiness
Calls Your Name

Channeled One-Minute Meditations
to Rewire Your Brain

Lorrie Kazan

Mystic Mind
Press

ISBN-10: 0692341269
ISBN-13: 978-0692341261

Book Design: Victor Osaka

Cover Art: ©2014 TrueLight Digital
Cover image available as a print. Contact victor@TrueLightDigial.com

To Rover, Magic, and Amber
whose luminous souls set the path of love ablaze
and taught me what it means to live from the heart.

Praise For Happiness Calls Your Name

"*Happiness Calls Your Name* is a fabulous book of poetic meditations for your soul. Filled with cheery metaphors to light up your life, Lorrie takes you on a journey that will fill your life with bliss—or remind you of the bliss you already possess. I'm loving reading this!"

— **Chellie Campbell**, author *The Wealthy Spirit* and *From Worry to Wealthy*

"Lorrie Kazan, a world renowned intuitive, has set forth magic in her book with a beauty, elegance and sensitivity she is sharing to help you join her in seeing, feeling and creating the energy of joy, love, happiness, peace of mind, prosperity and Light... the energies of a life well lived!"

— **Averi Torres**, Global Spiritual Advisor to many Presidents and World Leaders, Malibu's Resident Psychic.

"This book is a true gem in which Lorrie's soulful wisdom lovingly guides you toward your own."

— **Laura Alden Kamm**, author of *Intuitive Wellness*

"Joyful poetry for seekers of light and peace. So fun, beautiful and uplifting. I felt healed and inspired just reading. Thank you, Lorrie."

— **Diane Goldner**, author of *How People Heal* and *Called to Heal*

"Often, I receive guidance via a scattering of delicious 'Yes' tingles on the surface of my skin, communicating 'This is important. This is good. This is truth'. The poems and feeling-exercises Lorrie shares in this book make that happen bigtime for me. Even if reading and practicing these are all you ever do for your spiritual wellbeing, you'll experience a beautiful, positive shift in your life."

— **Naomi Janzen**, creator of the Remindfulness App and co-creator/co-host at OneMindLive.com

"There's a powerful spark of spirit, a unique creativity behind Lorrie's meditations. You can tell from their energy that she intentionally groomed her consciousness to the greatest degree of refinement possible, and set the intention that something might come forth from love, truth and beauty that would serve her readers. The results are a testament to that intent. They represent the reality of living truth. On a daily basis, I read many excerpts from channeled information. What Lorrie does deserves a new name because it's so far beyond it."

— **Dr. Henry Reed**, Director, Edgar Cayce Institute for Intuitive Studies, Professor, Atlantic University and author

Preface

This book represents my solution to problems my clients and I faced and had to overcome in order to lead richer, happier and more successful lives.

In writing, recording, and sharing my affirmations and meditations, my life began to soar. I made more money, had better luck, didn't feel sick all the time. When I shared them with my newsletter list, my subscribers claimed many of the same benefits.

The late psychoanalyst June Singer said she realized that it wasn't just she who was longing for the soul, but her soul that longed for her.

That's where I prefer to live now, in the soul that longed for me. Some people call this God-consciousness.

It's a place of tremendous light, which of course is still graced by shadow. It's my hope that these affirmations-meditations will remind you of the deeper truth that longs for you.

As you and I remember who we are, we begin to rise up, and to see with a more luminous perspective. A perspective that leads us where we want to go...

I invite you to contact me and let me know who you are and where you are in your journey. To enrich your process, please visit my website. I'm always adding more resources, such as articles, workshops, book reviews, and soon, a free Intuitive Living course. Plus, a recorded version of this book will be available for download.

Lorrie Kazan
Redondo Beach, California

lorrie@lorriekazan.com
www.ilovemypsychic.com

Foreword

We have an amazing capacity to create joy in our lives. But joy doesn't come by chance—joy is a choice. We must consciously wire our brains for joy.

In this gem of a book, Lorrie gives us the tools to help us cultivate our joy response. As an intuitive who helps others find harmony and beauty, she reminds us about our expansive capacities for trust, faith, and joy.

Lorrie's work is sorely needed. If you are like most everyone on the planet today, you probably feel the pressures of stress and anxiety. Who can think about joy when there are traffic jams, dental appointments, broken hearts, and worse? It's easy to let anxiety take the driver's seat—but we can choose a different path.

A look at the findings of neuroscience helps us understand why we need to develop our capacity for joy. Neuroscientists have discovered that human brains have a *default mode*. While at rest, your brain is busy doing four things—all without your asking it to do so:

First, your brain points out what's wrong with the present moment. In an attempt to make life better, the default mode criticizes rather than finds the good in what you are hearing, seeing, feeling, and doing.

Second, your brain time travels. Based on the painful events that happened to you in the past, your brain tries to protect you by predicting how you might be hurt again in the future. Mostly, your brain remembers the dangers in order to keep you safe.

Third, your brain works hard to construct your sense of self and give you a solid identity—"I am the kind of person who…" "The things I like are…" "What I don't like is…" and "People should treat me better because…" are statements it's constantly trying to complete. As a result, you may feel that life does not give you your due.

Lastly, your brain thinks about other people. It wonders what people think about you, what you think about them. It creates categories like Friend or Foe. And it compares you to others—"Is this person doing better than I am?" or "Do they have more than I do?"

These four functions of the default mode are the result of an evolutionary adaptation for survival. Found to be present in people of all cultures across the globe, the brain's default mode increased our ancestors' survival advantage and spurred their psychological development. But this is no longer the case. What once served us well now traps us in a competitive mode and activates our stress circuits.

By focusing on what's wrong with the present moment, with other people, and with our ourselves, the brain's default mode creates suffering.

Clearly, it's time to take charge of our lives in a new way. It's time to intervene consciously, to interrupt these competitive and fear-driven survival circuits and focus on building and strengthening our cooperative joy circuits.

Lorrie's poetic affirmations are the perfect antidote to the brain's default mode. Her words take us on a journey. Under her guidance, we soar with inspiration, calm down into contemplation. She wishes for us to find the inner rewards of feeling emotionally nurtured and spiritually connected. Her mystical generosity increases our capacity to trust the essential goodness of a loving universe that has our well-being at heart.

Lorrie's words teach us that we have agency and choice in how we focus our awareness. She coaches us to believe in love and abundance, to express caring, to cooperate with each other, to look with loving eyes.

Read these poems. Read them quietly or out loud to a loved one. Shout them from your back porch. Lorrie's book points us toward a new way of being. The skills in positive thinking and caring empathy she helps us practice are the essence of transformative healing for ourselves, for our relationships, and for our planet.

Dr. Aline LaPierre
Los Angeles

Coauthor of the best-selling book
Healing Developmental Trauma:
How Early Trauma Affects Self-Regulation,
Self-Image, and the Capacity for Relationship

www.DrAlineLaPierre.com

How To Use This Book

Initially, I would have loved to title this book, *How to Lose 10 Pounds, Look Better, and Be Smarter without Ever Having to Get Out of Bed*. Thus, supporting my fantasy of riding around town on a motorized bed, stocked with animals, books, snacks, and whatever else I fancied.

I work as a professional psychic and have been chosen as one of the top psychics by The Edgar Cayce Institute (The Association for Research and Enlightenment). Edgar Cayce was one of the most documented psychics in history.

You could call me a right-brained, creative type, someone who likes to and does work through the ethers, one who creates from where I am without having to rush out and slay dragons. Some people call this the feminine approach, in which we draw resources to us and shift reality from our core.

Happiness Calls Your Name will take you through this organic process, working from the inside out. "The journey of a thousand miles starts with a single step," said the ancient philosopher, Lao Tzu. First comes the concept of steps, and then the body can follow.

Years ago, I took a communication course where I was asked to "Create Creating." That is, conceive the notion that you can conceive ideas. This is largely how this book works, as well: begin by opening yourself to what might be possible whether you believe it or not.

How To Begin

You can start at page one. Or ask the universe to guide you to the right page and then, just open and read. That's your guidance for the day, or your mantra until you choose another. When I'm having a hard day, I just read through the book and something changes within me. Things begin to change around me; this can happen in your world, as well.

It's said that we see the world as we are rather than as it is. When you use these channeled meditations, your world is likely to become brighter, happier and attract more beauty.

You may find yourself feeling innately more patient and loving. *Happiness Calls Your Name* speaks to who you really are and clears out what doesn't belong.

What if you read one meditation and want just a little more light? Read another, or combine a few. Sit down later and see how they changed your experience.

Keep it simple. We lose ourselves in complexity. You never have to be something you're not. You were designed for this world and it was designed for you. For most of my early life, my non-stop question was, "Where is my place in this world?" Using these tools helped me connect my train to a track that took me in a direction my soul needed and wanted to go.

You can do as little or as much as you like with this book. Ponder or write about how these words and images, these vibrations, could alter your day. You can ask yourself, "If I really believed that the spiritual truths in these meditations were real, what might I be doing, saying or being today?" And notice if you're doing that.

If you prefer a more classic meditation structure:

Sit up, with your back straight, feet flat on the floor, hands upon your lap, eyes looking upward and eyelids closed. Repeat a line or say some of the words in your head. Let your mind simply follow it, or get lost in it. You can even be with it for a set amount of time (set a timer) and when it goes off, you're done!

The only way you could use this book wrong would be not to use it at all. It's a book of solutions in poetic prose, arranged so the brain can grasp and then use these words to replace some of the old negative tapes most of us have rolling around, tapes we may be unaware we play.

How will doing this solve your problems? The old adage says, spend 20% of your energy on the problem, 80% on solution. None of us needs any more lessons on how to feel badly about ourselves or anything else.

It's said that pain is part of life, but suffering (self-torturing) is optional. I'm asking you to surrender, or be willing to surrender that option, at least for the time you entertain yourself here.

These words are imbued with spiritual truth, the foundation that's under us all. You are a brilliant soul, a diamond of light clothed in human form. The more you welcome this truth, the greater your access to your soul. The more your inner self begins to trust you, the more it will interact, share its secrets and its unending source of love.

You can use this book anywhere, including the comfort of your own bed, looking out from a mountaintop, or waiting your turn at the DMV.

It was written so you could run your wild way, even sit slumped if you desired (though you won't after you've done enough of these).

Yell them into the forest, or out loud in your car; say them in your head in the midst of chaos. Read them upon awakening, or before sleep; pull them out of your knapsack, pocketbook, Gucci bag…whatever helps you say *yes* to these crystalline words that are all about your success.

You'll find it's easy, effective, and works if you work it. Live with it, think it, say it, and engage with the ideas. The more you use this book, the more you will realize from it. Plant these seeds. Feed yourself positive loving thoughts and do it again and again. You will reap what you sow.

What if you get tested? What if you encounter pain, or something along the road that makes you mad, regretful, or distracted? Continue playing this new game, keep calling in and living the divine truth. Patience is a powerful friend to cultivate.

I now grant you the right to be who you are, presuming you're not a psychopath. (And even then you can still be who you are; just opt for medical supervision.)

You have the right to feel loved, no matter your circumstances. You won the genetic lottery; you are here. Claim the path that is your divine right. Its vibration calls to you, just as yours calls to it. Welcome home. You've been missed.

Notes

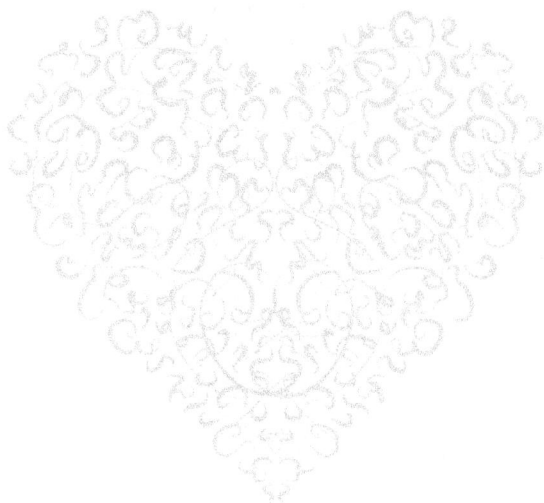

Safe In This World

When the world is on stilts or the flying trapeze,
you might feel so worried you drop to your knees.
You call out for safety but there's none to be seen.
Everything's spinning, rearranging your dreams.
Over and over the world seems to fall.
Where is the net that's under us all?

When the world is on stilts or the flying trapeze,
you might feel tossed like a ship in rough seas.
Then you remember…the world loves a spin.
It loves to upend and right itself again.
If over and over you seek inner peace,
in the midst of chaos you're bound to find ease.

For Today

Seek inner peace.

Notes

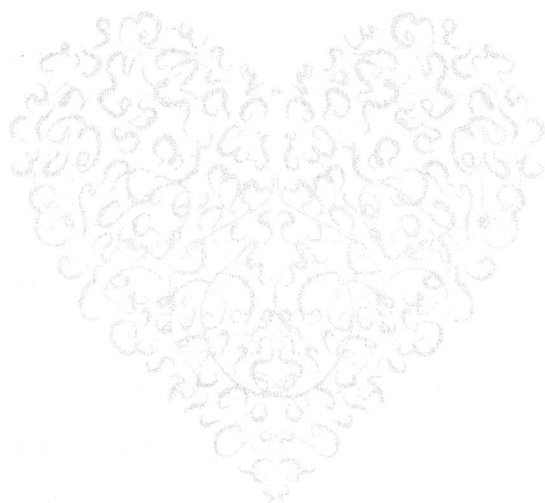

Miracles Come My Way

Miracles come my way,

like a lamp that shines and seems to say,

all that you seek is here, please stay.

Eternity wraps me in its wings,

comforts me with tender whisperings.

Tomorrow brings another day,

another chance to learn new ways.

Ships, whipped by the wind,

disappear and sail back again.

For Today

Imagine the beauty of ships sailing safely on the sea.

Notes

My Soul Has The Power

It rattles the windows and blows out the doors;

the power of my being brilliantly soars forth.

Yes is the answer, *yes* is the way;

my soul has the power and it has its own say.

For Today

Repeat throughout the day:
"My soul has the power and has its own say."

Notes

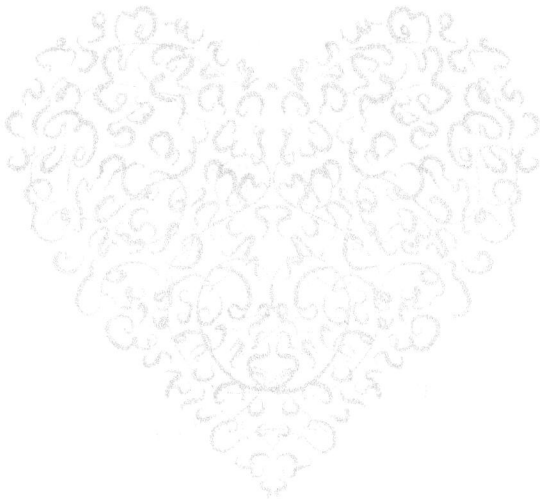

Miracles You May Not See

I open my arms to hug the sky
for all the stars that light the night,
for the daylight sun that warms my bones,
for a place to sleep I call my home.
I give thanks for all the good that comes to me,
for tiny miracles I may not see.
I give thanks I can receive.
Even on an average day
I am so much luckier than I can say.

For Today

Find something simple to be grateful for.
If you can't, then imagine one small thing
you'd like to be grateful for.

Notes

All The Riches I Need

All the riches I need are now mine to claim.

All the wishes that free me...just enter this way.

Called forth by laughter, I cannot resist.

I punched in my ticket for this streetcar called bliss.

I love every minute because now life is play.

I love myself for taking time this way.

All the riches I need are now mine to claim.

All the wealth I wished for...now bears my name.

For Today

Proclaim your good.

Notes

This Joyous Day

Divine love takes my breath away,

it radiates through my soul

and moves me gently from night to day.

Life is good and I am free.

Every wonderful opportunity is now open for me.

As I say *yes* to all the best, even better comes my way.

I am rich in everything that matters

and fully present in this joyous day.

For Today

Feel free.
Breathe it in deeply.

Notes

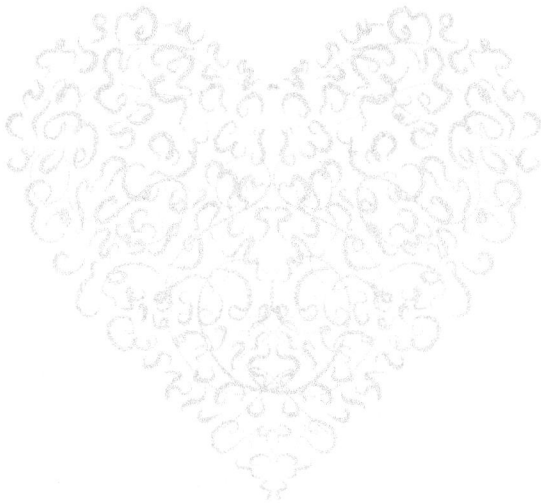

I Create The Life I Dream

That which is meant for me readily comes to be.

Every day, in every way,

I allow myself to make whatever change my soul craves.

Even if I stand apart, I take the risks that heal my heart,

and I create the life I dream.

For Today

Dream.

Notes

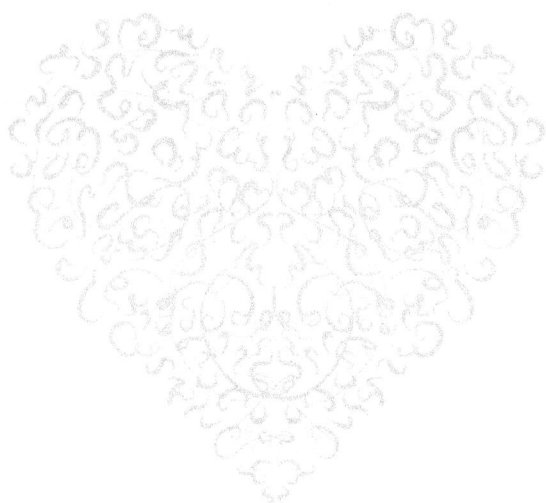

Enfolded In Grace

Enfolded in grace,

my divine right place is forever an image in Go(o)d.

It's there for me whether or not I see.

I am essential as the birds and trees,

the rain, the sun and the summer breeze.

Created in light, converging in love,

we are so much more than we seem.

Today I believe I can have even my deepest dreams.

For Today

Rest in the divine arms of grace.

Notes

Infinite Success

The earth is a blaze of light

and every being bathed in luminosity.

I tap into the source of wealth (and well-being)

and am rewarded over and over again.

Spirit flows generously.

My needs are met with ease.

I am guided and I am blessed.

Every day I breathe is an infinite success.

For Today

Breathe in infinite success.

Notes

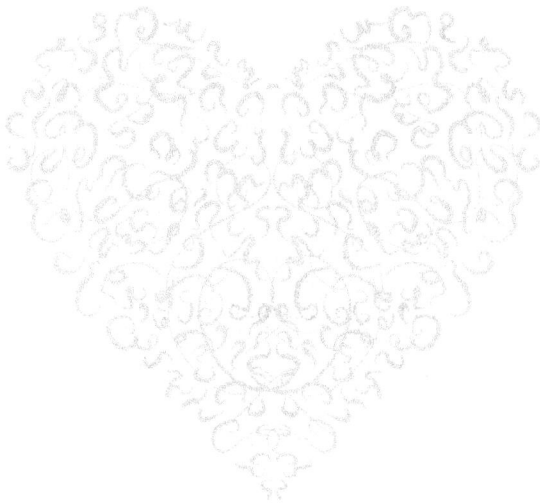

Alive In Consciousness

The light of good showers me in bliss.

I am alive in consciousness.

The path beneath my feet,

like the breath of stars, emboldens me.

I, too, am made of stars.

That stellar core is in my bones

I am meant for more than I could ever do alone.

The light of good showers me in bliss

as I am reborn in willingness.

I let go of what I know and allow my heart to see.

For Today

See yourself showered in radiant energy.

Notes

Your Breath Skips A Beat

I flow like a petal cascading on the breeze.

I am in harmony with all that I see,

and deeply nourished by everything.

The world is luminous with the joy of my being.

I have permission to savor it all.

Even the simplest moment fills me with awe.

All that I am is divinely inspired,

as if the world were a bouquet of millions of flowers.

I am carried by the bliss of it all.

For Today

Just imagine a petal
floating freely on the breeze.

Notes

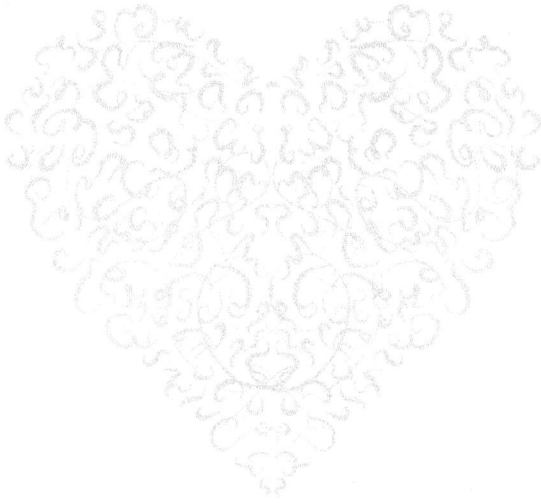

I Am Blessed
Beyond Consciousness

I am blessed beyond all levels of consciousness.

The infinite force inside each flower and tree

is the same breath that stirs within me.

I cherish the land beneath my feet,

and treat each moment as aspects of divinity.

All that I need comes to me perfectly timed

and completely aligned

to my highest destiny.

For Today

Let your feet sense the ground beneath them.

Notes

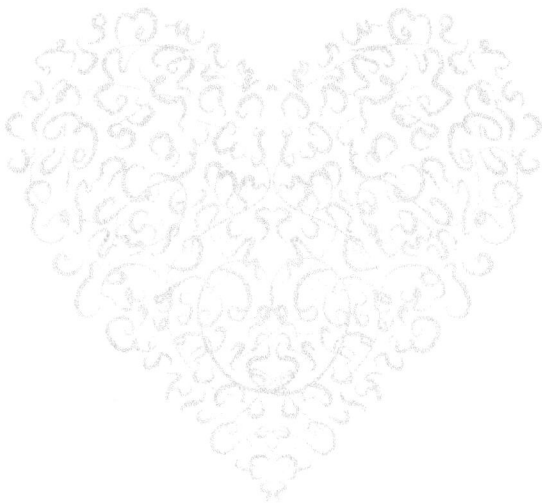

My Heart Sees

This miraculous day inspires me in ingenious ways.
It opens my heart
to see beyond judgments
and allows me to live from my soul.
I am on an adventure like I've never known.
This miraculous day carries me
to heights in ways that expand the good of who I am,
and lead to the enrichment of everyone.

For Today

Breathe into your heart.

Notes

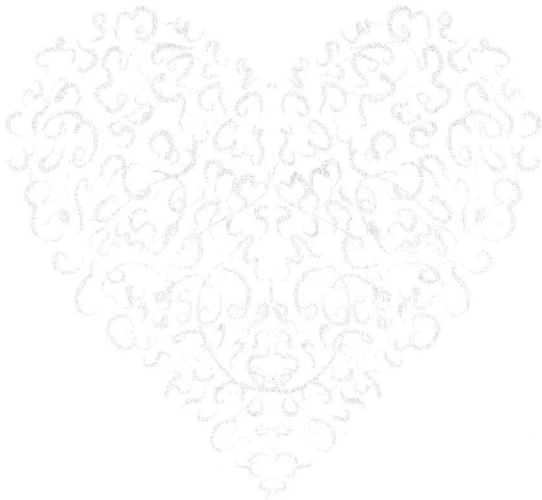

It's A New Day

It's a new day, filled with love, adventure,
excitement and play.
Goodbye old worries, ways of being,
illnesses, and thought forms.
Goodbye to the ways I've seen things.
Everything now contributes to my well-being
and intimately enhances my deepest dreams.

For Today

Close your eyes and breathe into your dreams.

Notes

Fear Falls Away

Today, I open to joy and play.

I focus on blessings, and fears fall away.

I forgive and forgive, and I am forgiven as well.

Gaining freedom and pleasure

as the past becomes the glorious Now…

Light and fun and filled with pleasure for everyone.

For Today

Forgive something or someone.

Notes

The Earth Sings In Flowers

The earth sings in flowers,

convinces me with trees

that life is so much greener than I believed it would be.

In this world of possibility,

I am humbled beneath a canopy of stars

that keep the night at bay,

and guide me so gently on my right way.

I too am made of stars,

and nature's plan for me

is so much greater than my eyes can see.

For Today

Notice flowers.

Notes

Already Always Mine

Doors open wherever I go.

The Universe loves to say *Yes*.

Divine whisper becomes clear intention,

and every action rightly aimed.

I live fully, in greatest love and well-being.

The more I give, the more I receive.

I am always where I am meant to be,

having the divine right experience designed for me.

For Today

Imagine the doors of your life opening.

Notes

Everything I Do
Opens Me To Something New

Everything I do unveils something new.

As adventures abound,

opportunities are even found in toughest times.

Everything I do opens me to something new

and expands the good of who I am.

I now let whatever I see create more love

and acceptance inside of me.

For Today

Accept this moment just as it is.

Notes

I Breathe In
This Glorious Day

I breathe in this glorious day.

Even when it doesn't look the way I think it should,

I know all things work together for good.

I surrender to the play of the birds on the passionate sea.

I watch gulls dive ferociously

as sun burns its way across the cloud-scattered sky.

Suddenly I realize that all the love that ever was

is already always mine.

For Today

Imagine all the love that ever was
is already always yours.

Notes

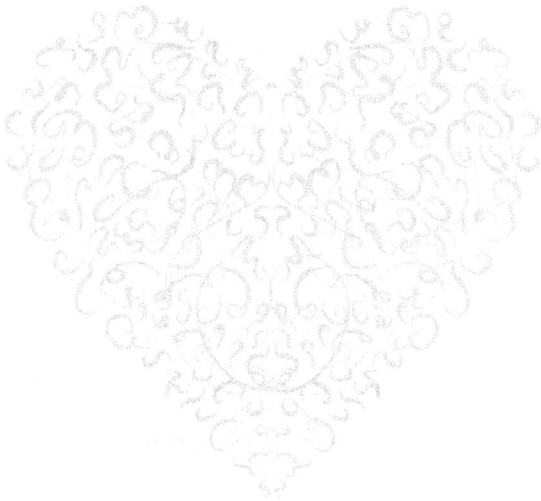

Inner Peace Is Born In Me

In the light of all that is, in the midst of everything,
inner peace is born in me—
a sense of oneness with the divine.
I am safe inside my skin, inside this life
where tranquility reigns supreme.
I rest within this changing dream
where inner peace is destiny.

For Today

Breathe inner peace.

Notes

My Life Is A Gift
Too Spectacular To Miss

Spirit's perfection sweeps me in its divine right direction,

where I am at peace, complete and serene.

Surrounded by beauty, infused in love,

gratitude and generosity are my guides.

My life is a gift too exquisite to miss.

For Today

Appreciate one thing.

Notes

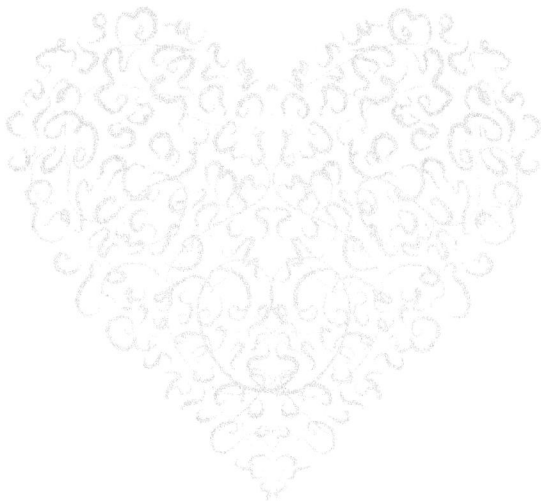

The Silver Light That Shimmers On The Sea

The silver light that shimmers on the sea
is no less dazzling
than the light that emanates from within me.
All the good that ever was wants me to succeed,
all the love that's ever been
now lives bountifully in me.

For Today

*Imagine all the good that ever was
wants you to succeed.*

Notes

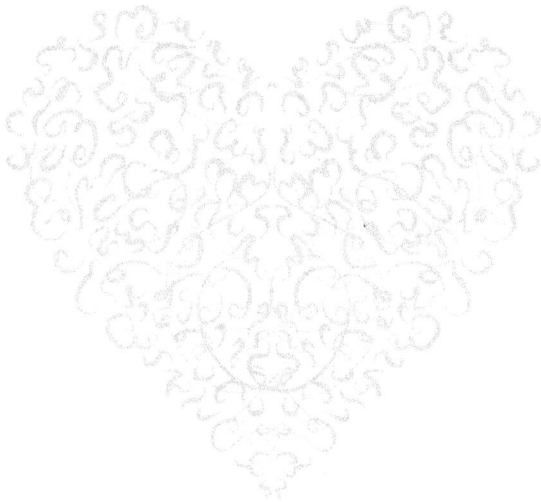

You Are Worthy

Like a leaf in motion, or petals flying free,

I am one with everything, no matter how it seems.

I feel myself inside my skin,

I feel the earth beneath my feet,

I know myself as someone worthy of all I am meant to be.

I am a mix of blessings in a rainbow called me.

For Today

You are all you're meant to be.

Notes

Laughter Flows

I am blessed, I am blessed, I am blessed,
and I release all the rest.
Laughter flows as I affirm what I know
that all is well in my world.
Well-being springs from my core.
It rises above circumstances
and creates more of my inner intention:
peace and harmony prevail.

For Today

Smile, even if it's the smallest tweak of your lips.

Notes

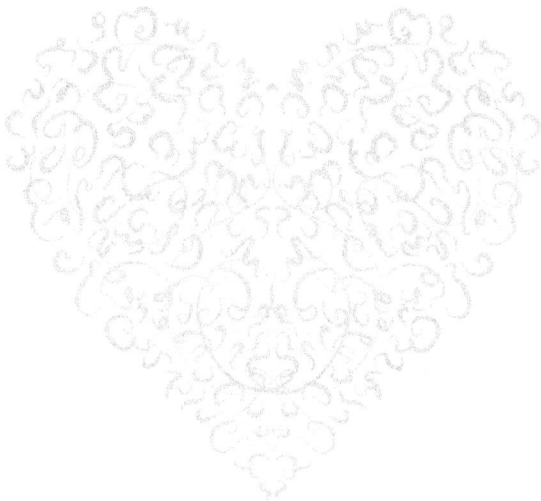

Pause to Dream

The sun through the clouds lights a bridge on the sea,

mirrors of gold, dazzling and free,

holding a promise as if to say,

you who have come so far, weary traveler,

pause to dream.

You, who have left your mother's womb,

find your true source in me.

Lay down your armor, let go your sword.

As night touches day so your dreams will soar forth.

For Today

Pause.
If it's a hectic day, pause a little more often.

Notes

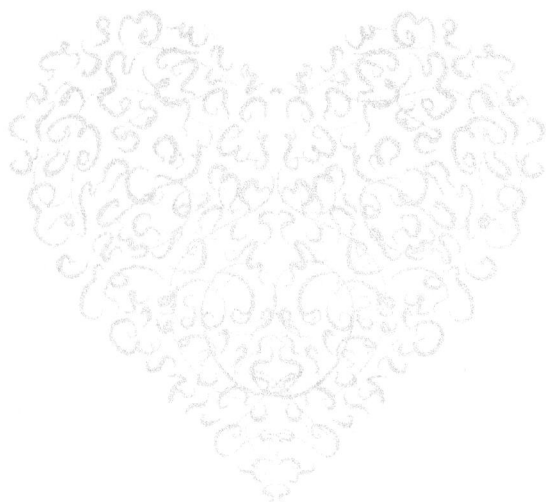

Poet And The Poem

I am the poet and the poem,
the breath of God being born.
I am everything I'm meant to be
for the precious life that lives through me.

For Today

You are the weaver of your life's tapestry.
Step back and admire your art.

Notes

The World Is An Embrace

This world is an embrace.

Everywhere I go I am safe, welcome and well received.

Beauty surrounds me, generosity abounds around me.

I am lavishly paid to do what I love

and rich beyond my dreams.

Happy, healthy, and exuberantly free,

I easily express the joy that's within me.

The more I give, the more I receive.

Life continually prospers me.

For Today

Say thank you, to yourself, to the universe.
Thank You.

Notes

A Loving Presence

If butterflies are divine, then so are we.
Today I choose to see the good in everything.
In any situation, no matter how it seems,
I affirm a loving presence guiding me to my dreams.
The wind that whirls the leaves and breathes through trees
is no more, no less divine than you or me.
Today I see the prospering power of nature
driving everything.

For Today

Tune into the abundance that already is.
Look at nature if you need inspiration.

Notes

Abundance Is Already Mine

This glorious day
is filled with joy in so many ways.
As my heart opens to delight and play,
abundance is already mine.

For Today

Notice an area of abundance…anywhere.

Notes

Kindness

Kindness greets me on baby feet,

soft as angels' wings and petal-sweet.

Entering my heart like wisps of air,

I am uplifted and inspired

without knowing where the sense of peace began.

I only know it's here.

For Today

Close your eyes and breathe in kindness.

Notes

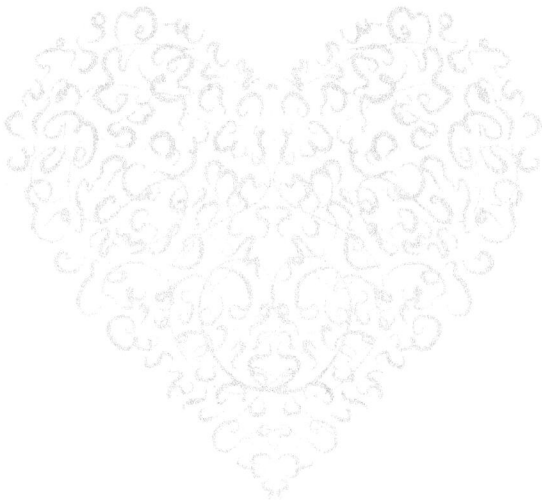

My Heart's Desire

Cradled inside a glowing light,

the heart opens and dreams take flight,

joining the stars that blanket the night.

They shimmer, *yes yes*, to each perfect plan of success.

Yes, today my heart's desire is fully met.

For Today

Breathe in love and well-being.

Notes

Cells Of Light

Every cell is filled with light and like an inner guide
it leads me right.
Even in the darkest night, all is well in my world.
Every step I take
leaves boundless good fortune in its wake.
Even money comes to me in great big quantities.
So much good accrues that all I can do
is share it freely, live it fully,
and watch it increase tenfold.

For Today

Let the good in your life increase tenfold.

Notes

Good Fortune Loves Me

Good fortune loves me, can't get enough of me,

cozies up to where I sleep,

fills my heart to overflow;

even money accumulates wherever I go.

The powers that be make a positive example out of me.

For Today

Breathe in this meditation...
Let it fill your bones.

Notes

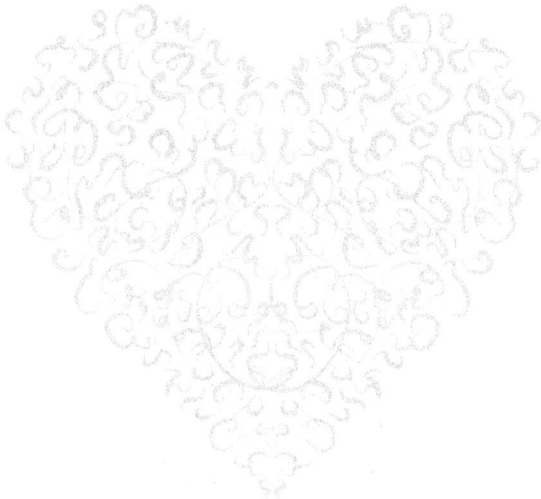

My Perfect Path

There is a path that calls to me

and shines out like no other.

It twists and turns,

it looks wrong one day, and perfectly aligned another.

My feet seek this golden road

as if they've walked this way before.

As I follow the path of the heart,

I'm led to each right door.

For Today

Imagine walking the golden path,
doors opening and light flooding through.

Notes

Weaving The World Anew

Each small step opens waves of change.
Every smart action weaves the world anew.
Every day I chip away at becoming who I am.
The past slips into a cold, black sea
where it now slumbers into eternity.
The future reaches out and grabs my hand,
"Come on" it says,
and leads me into the life I planned.

For Today

Imagine waves...waves of change.

Notes

Higher Order
Creates My Dreams

I am guided by an overwhelming sense of success.

No matter how it seems,

higher order is always carving out my dreams.

I embrace and know that love and abundance

are everywhere I go.

For Today

Repeat this as a mantra:
"Higher Order Creates My Dreams!"

Notes

Today Is A Mystery

Today is a mystery, freeing me to create

whatever history my soul craves.

My mind revels in this precise moment in time.

Every second is sacred, every breath easily taken.

I am lucky, happy and joyful,

I now welcome this ongoing season of well-being.

For Today

Say, throughout the day:
"I am lucky."

Notes

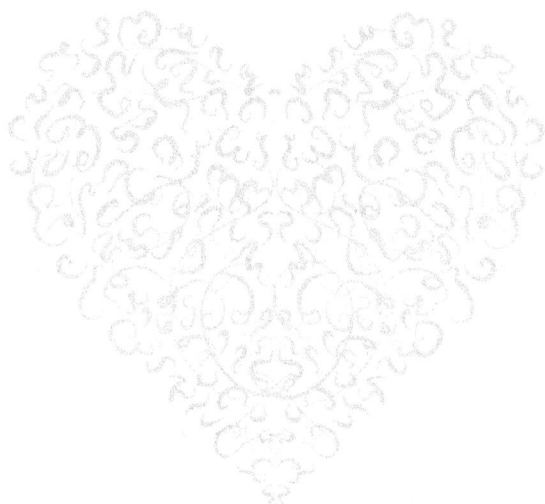

Love Comes To Me

Love comes to me from everywhere it knows how to be.

As end of night awakens day,

so loving thoughts bring more and more love my way.

Life is rich and fulfilling.

I feel it with every breath I draw in.

I am safe and sound.

Beauty abounds and abundance reigns over all.

For Today

Be gentle with yourself and others.

Notes

Blessings Rain Upon Me

Blessings rain down upon me.

I am bathed in the beauty of this day.

Miracles, big and small, take my breath away.

Everywhere I look new life begins.

The earth is ablaze in love

and speaks in mountains, valleys and streams.

For Today

Notice miracles, however small.

Notes

My Open Heart

My open heart drinks in the purest light from my Source.

Spontaneous joy breezes through me,

and emanates to my core.

Every resource flows freely,

providing infinite options intricately timed.

For Today

Allow.
Allow feelings to move through you.

Notes

I Live Inside
The Breath Of Love

I embrace stillness as if it were my dream.

I carry it inside me and no matter how things seem,

I live inside the breath of love,

a place where nothing but the divine is real.

As I let it fill my heart,

it creates boundless miracles.

For Today

Remind yourself often:
I let inner stillness lead the way.

Notes

Good Comes To Me

Good comes to me, great things come from me.

My path is a blaze of light

imbued with everything I need to live the life I dream.

I fill myself to overflow

with loving actions that continue to grow.

I send peace to every being.

All are forgiven

and this day starts anew.

For Today

Take a loving action.

Notes

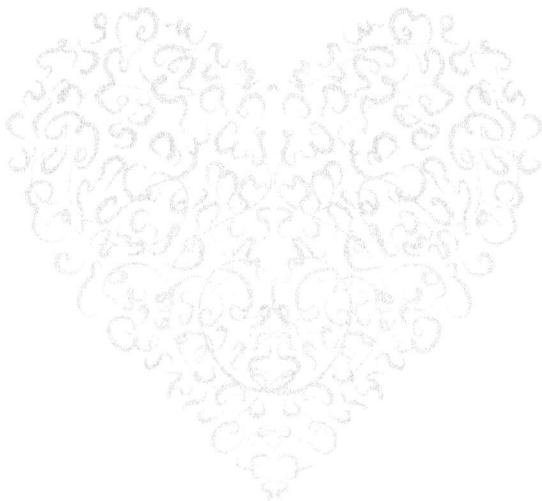

The Wonder Of Yes

I am free. I am at peace.

I am where I am meant to be.

I cherish the miraculous energy that has entered

the world as me.

I am the flower inside the seed,

searching for beauty, for what it can be.

I am the acorn that becomes the oak.

All that I see is in my own growth.

I am the flower, the tree, the moon, and its beams.

For Today

You are free.

Notes

I Swim In A Sea Of Well-Being

I swim in a sea of well-being. I release the past
and let feelings of love last longer than any other.
My cells drink in the purest light from the source.
I radiate health and divine inspiration.
I am truly blessed with a sacred sense of worthiness.
All that I need is here for me.
All that I am is more than I can see.
I trust the loving Universe to fulfill my deepest dreams.

For Today

Imagine floating...
imagine floating through this world, just for today.

Notes

Compassion Is My Guide

Compassion is my guide and inner peace my destiny.

All is as it's meant to be.

With each and every breath,

I allow the deepest part of me

to rest in higher consciousness.

All is as it's meant to be

for the abundant life meant for me.

For Today

All is as it's meant to be...however it is,
and however it isn't.

Notes

My Deepest Dreams Come True

Floating like a feather on the breath of the divine,
one with presence, empowered by infinite mind.
Awe and wonder inspire and guide.
As each kind thought and loving action
flood the world with higher vibration,
my deepest dreams come true.

For Today

Say throughout the day:
"My deepest dreams come true."

Notes

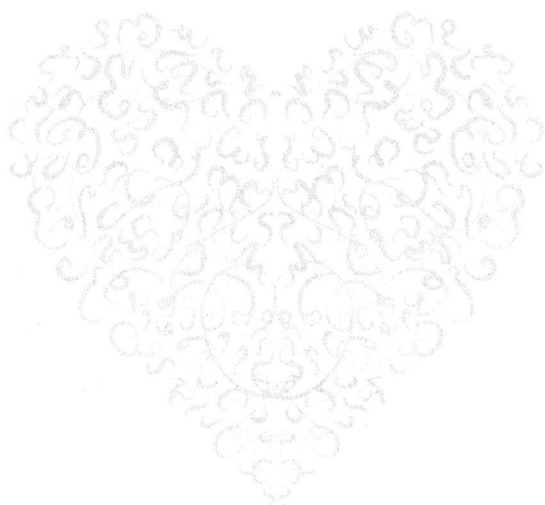

Kindness Leads The Way

Today, kindness leads the way.

It opens doors I thought were blocked

and those I hadn't seen.

It lets me belong to every person, place, plant and tree.

And allows all beings to resonate with me.

It feeds the soul with depth and light.

It lets my bodymind select what's right,

and abundance flow with ease.

For Today

Contemplate kindness.
Speak gently to yourself.

Notes

Life Is A Dancer

Today, as judgments slip away,

life becomes play.

Rhythms of the earth rise through my feet.

Life is a dancer with its hand out to me.

Every footfall and twirl, each nonsensical spin

allows the music to become new again.

For Today

See your life as a dance in motion.

Notes

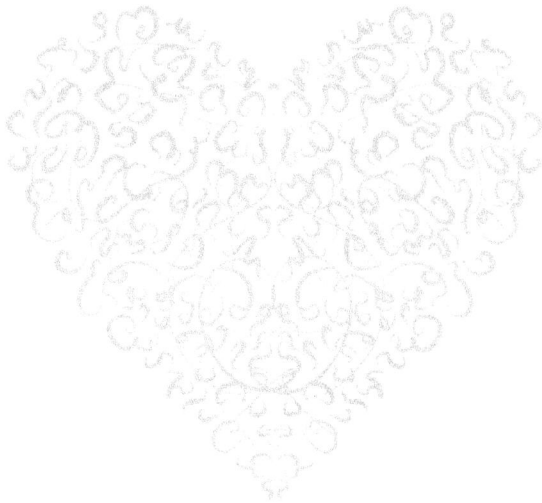

My Inner Light Shines

I allow my inner light to shine,

radiating good fortune from deep inside.

Wild birds wing through the sky,

reminding me I have my own way to fly.

I am one with all that is and the grandeur that will be.

Of all the stars that light the night,

there's none so special or half so bright as me.

For Today

Feel the freedom of the wild birds as they fly.

Notes

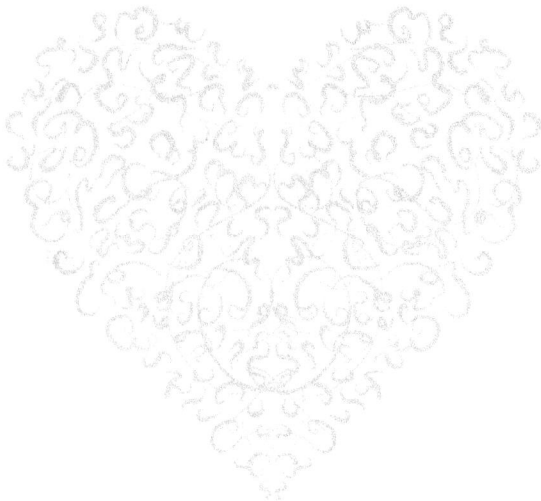

One Small Drop

Small as a drop in the ocean, so minute it can't be seen.

Still I trust the divine working through me,

creating what the world needs.

I am one small drop in an enormous sea,

yet the ocean would be missing something vital

if it were not for me.

For Today

Let yourself be an essential drop in the ocean of life.

Notes

Compassion In Every Cell

Kindness carries me as if I were a child.

Compassion fills every cell.

I overflow with love and radiate dynamic health.

For Today

Let compassion overflow.

Notes

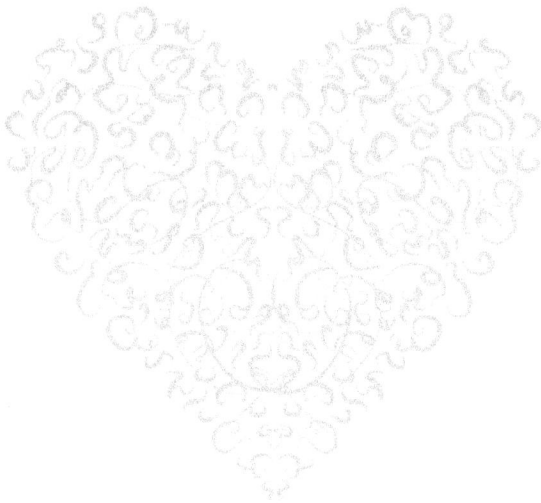

The Symphony I Am

As I dwell in bliss,

I release fears of unworthiness.

The symphony I am is created by divine plan.

The Notes that sound from my soul make me deeply whole.

I am love in action. I am light in motion.

I am whom I'm meant to be.

I now claim the great fortune meant for me.

For Today

See yourself as light in motion.

Notes

Whatever I Need Is Given

Each and every day, abundance flows my way.

I swim in a stream of well-being

and bask in divine flow.

Whatever I need is given, I need never fear letting go.

For Today

Bask in divine flow.

Notes

All Are One

I am one with the stars in the sky, the bells that ring,

the scent of roses wafting perfume in spring,

I am part of everything, the rain, the clouds,

the trees shedding leaves,

the wind that whirls the night away,

the morning sun proclaiming a new day.

I am one with everything,

the birds that chirp and sing, flowers sharing pollen,

I am one with all that is

and one with what will be.

For Today

Live with the notion that you are one with everything.

Notes

Abundance Is In My DNA

Divine essence is everywhere present,
expressing bountifully through me.
As I open to the splendor of this day,
life's gifts are revealed in numinous ways.
Abundance is in my DNA.
I am lucky at life, lucky at love,
and great health courses through my veins.

For Today

Say it freely:
"Abundance is in my DNA!"

Notes

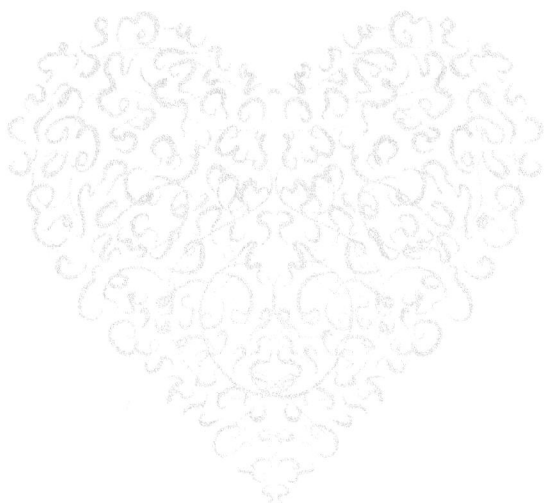

If All I Saw Were Flowers

If all I ever saw were flowers, how happy would I be?

Today I invest my thoughts in what truly matters to me.

The more I feed my soul, the greater bounty overflows.

What delights the heart will surely ease the mind.

Nothing has more beauty than a rose in its full flower.

No one has more riches than I in my full power.

For Today

Repeat often:
"What delights the heart will surely ease the mind!"

Notes

Now Is

Now is the only Is that is,

the one that dances a silly jig.

"Go out and play; I've had enough seriousness today."

Those are the words it wants to say.

Now is the most Is that is;

it moves so fast it can't be seen,

yet it unleashes joyous dreams.

Now is the only Is that is.

It can't be seen but must be lived.

For Today

Live in the Is whatever it is.

Notes

The Inner Voice

In the depth of everything, the inner voice begins to sing—
So loud, so clear, so true.
"Who are you?" asks the day-bright spring
The inner voice so loves to sing it finds its tune in everything.
Bird's wings, flowers, leaves, orange petals, stinging nettles.
The good, the bad, the in-between.
In the thick of everything, the inner voice learns how to sing
so loud, so clear, so true.
No matter whether night or day,
the inner voice now has its say.

For Today

Give your inner voice permission to sing.

Notes

Beauty

Beauty wells inside my soul, it's who I am, it's what I know.

It's in all the good that calls to me,

the sacred song I learn to sing.

It floats on the wind, ripples in streams, enfolds me in grace

and urges me to begin again and again.

For Today

Trust that beauty lives in you
and if you've given up on something, including yourself,
you can begin again.

Notes

State Of Mind

Today I choose my state of mind.
I pick happiness for this moment in time.

For Today

Notice your state of mind.

Notes

A Joke And A Half

Today is like a belly laugh,

a hardy—h-a-r—h-a-r,

a joke and a half.

It overflows with all-out fun,

outrageous giggles and love for everyone.

For Today

Remember a time when you giggled?
Keep your eyes out for giggling children.

Notes

Sharpest Me

The person I was meant to be now takes the reins
and speaks through me.
Powerful, peaceful, loving and smart,
sharpest player in the deck,
sharpest me I've ever met.
Go-getter, experienced meditator,
the one who says yes and no with sheer conviction,
uses time wisely, lives for a mission.
The truest me is all I wish to be.

For Today

Who do you wish to be?

Notes

A Whisper
On The Breath Of God

The power that creates the night, the day, the moon,

the stars and the ocean waves,

sways my path in bountiful ways.

Like a whisper on the breath of Go(o)d,

"This way," it says, its speech so soft.

If I hesitate, it says it again:

"Listen to the voice that speaks through the wind.

Track the feathers of the birds flying free.

Follow nature's path and you'll be following me."

For Today

Notice nature.

Notes

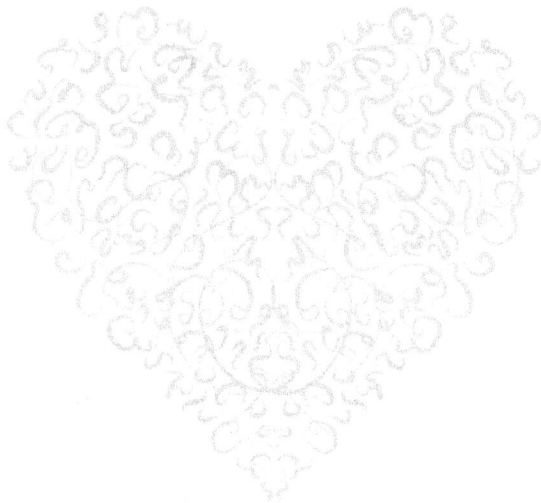

Beyond My Range

If I don't dance around the clock,
kick up my heels to a wild tick tock,
if I don't sing higher than I ought,
how will I know where I should really stop?
How will I know when I've reached the end?
The period not the comma,
the exclamation point that means *Wow*!
If I don't sing beyond my range,
how will I know what I'm capable of?

For Today

Go beyond your range.
For example, sing louder, walk one step farther,
write a poem, even a bad poem...

Notes

Yes

Gratitude wraps me in its wings,

warms me with tender whisperings

and tells me it all works out in the end.

I give thanks for good I've yet to see,

for all the good that calls to me,

like a song I don't yet know how to sing.

It floats on the wind, ripples on streams,

enfolds me in grace and encourages me to begin again.

For Today

Give thanks for something you want
even if you don't know how you'll receive it.

Notes

Free Day

Time slipped out the window or slid under the door,

I say goodbye to time because time exists no more.

No big tick tock of the big fake clock,

no schoolmarm shaking a fist.

Time slipped out the back and I now live in bliss.

For Today

Run free or do something that makes you feel free.

Notes

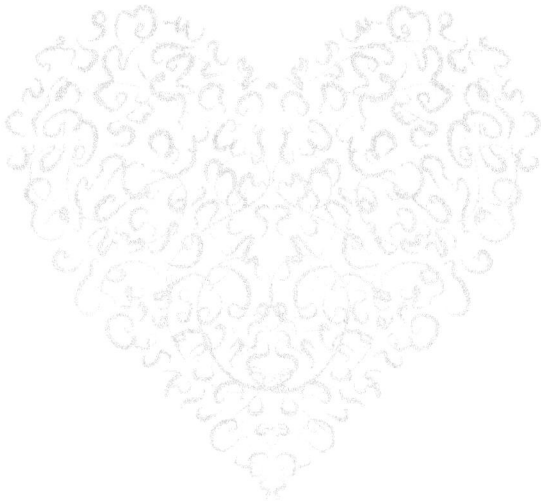

Wisdom

Wisdom finds its way to me,
it rules my heart and teaches bravery.
It finds humor in everything,
wraps itself around my dreams
and speaks to me from deep within.
All is as it's meant to be.
This is the life that's meant for me.

For Today

Repeat beyond what's needed:
"All is as it's meant to be,
creating more and more miracles is my perfect destiny."

Notes

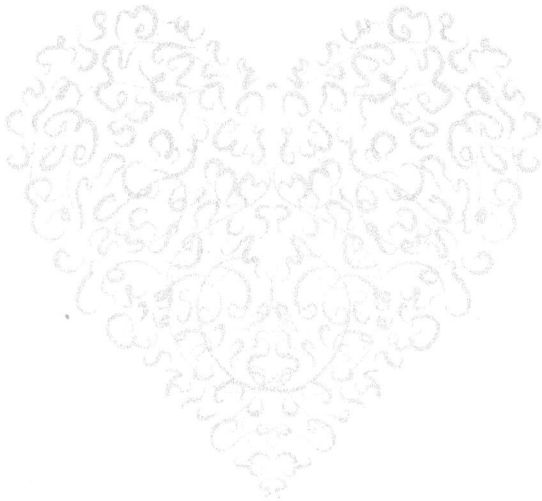

Success Is In My DNA

Success is in my DNA.

It calls my name.

Come out and play.

It says: "You are on the right path today.

Come take a chance. Do a crazy dance."

Success whirls through my DNA.

"Come break some rules. Come have your say."

Because success rules my DNA,

it knows the game I'm here to play.

It knows that all is right with me today.

For Today

Believe.

Notes

My Way Of Being

Today I laugh from deep within.

Ha, ha, ha becomes my way of being.

Ha, ha, ha is the song I sing.

Ha, ha, ha, ha is how my phone rings.

Laughter follows me everywhere.

It weaves itself inside my cares.

Today I wear my funny face, my inner jokes, my happy place.

The future is a load of laughs,

a big guffaw that slaps my back

and sends me merrily down the divine right path.

Today, I laugh and laugh.

For Today

Laugh.

Notes

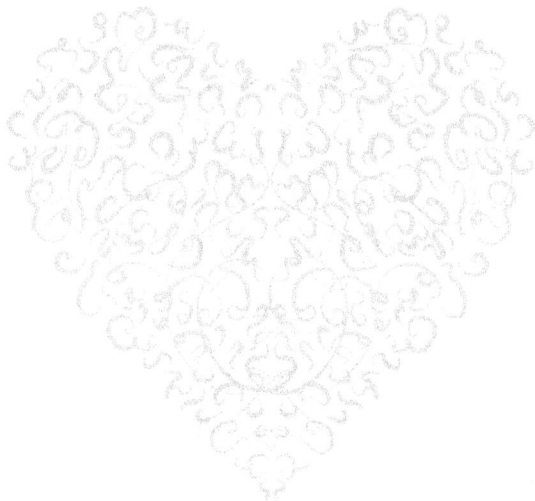

My Body Soaks Up
The Good Words I Say

This is a perfect day, filled with bliss in so many ways.

My body soaks up the good words I say,

and lets go of any other.

I am happy, healthy, abundant and free.

All my best affirmations work magnificently.

For Today

Let your body soak up positive thoughts and vibrations,
like a sponge drinking in healing waters.

Notes

Listen

There's a symphony among the trees,

fanned by every passing breeze.

Blue birds are the clarinets and hummingbirds the bells.

In the quiet of the moonlit night, the forest forms a call.

Insects are the tympani, fish find out they're flutes.

Bats keep the rhythm strong

and owls howl their inner Who.

The forest is alive in song; it sings for me and you.

It tells us that we're part of it,

and all we need to do is listen to the song inside.

Listen and stay true.

For Today

Stay true to something you love.

Notes

In The Garden Of The Senses

I live in the garden of the senses, a field of sheer delight,

where roses bloom and lilies dance,

and fireflies shed their light.

Dense with scents of every kind, from jasmine to chocolate mint,

fountains flow as birds soar high

and life is better than it's ever been.

For Today

Use your senses.
Smell a flower, listen closely, or close your eyes and see.

Notes

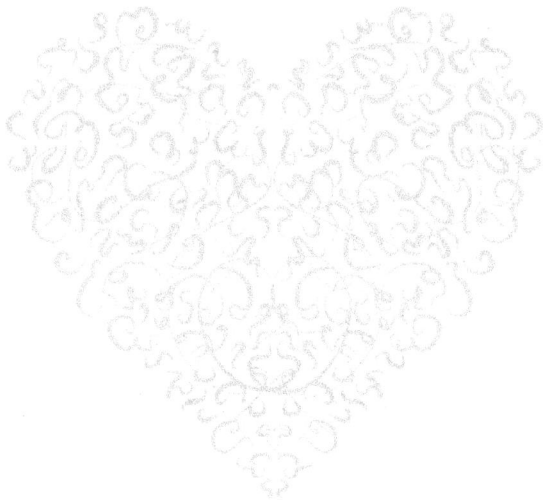

The Ideal Me

I am now the ideal me, as happy as happy can be.
I feed myself with truth and love
and inhale inner peace.
All my cells are laughing, giggling as they please.
I am now the ideal me, as free as free can be.

For Today

Feel free, if only for seconds at a time.

Notes

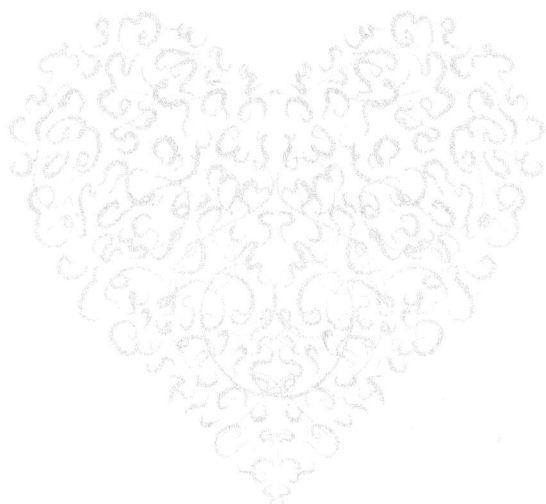

Better Self

Dear Better Self, come sit with me.
Bring all the spinning selves
that weave my personal tapestry.
Welcome all the Me's in me,
the good, the great, the in-between.
Welcome every thread I see.
Dear Better Selves, come play with me.

For Today

Imagine you're filled with selves, some you've yet to see.

Notes

Happiness Overflows

Happiness comes to me
from near and far, from land and sea,
from every corner where it could possibly be.
Arising from thin air,
it follows me everywhere, pulls up for joy rides,
honks its horn, peels back the roof
and reveals the sky.
Even on sad or lonely days, happiness finds a way to say:
"Wake up, wake up. Open to your life today."

For Today

What if you could be happy for no reason?
What if happy surprises were waiting to be seen?

Notes

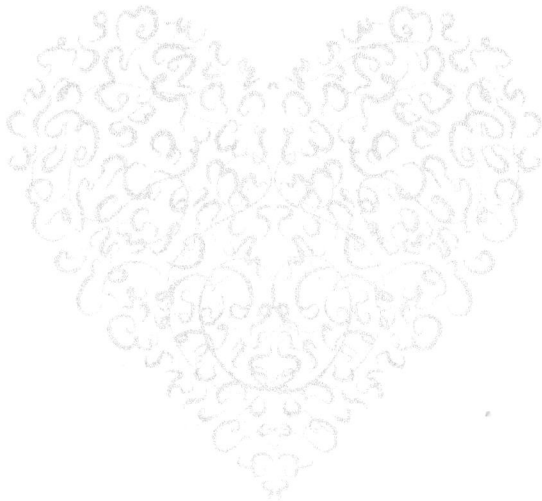

I Attract
What's Best For Me

Kindness is my destiny.

With it, I attract what's best for me.

Abundance flows with speed and ease.

Even money arrives in quantities beyond what I have seen.

All my deepest dreams come true,

in every day, in every way, no matter what I do.

For Today

Be kind.

Notes

All That Is

I am one with every fleeting thing:
the owl's call, the wind's howl, the starling chirping in a tree.
I am one with all that lives and all that breathes,
one with all that is and can't be seen.
One with every puff of air,
one with the earth and all it bears,
one with every heart that beats,
one with all that is and will ever be.

For Today

Imagine you are one with nature.

Notes

The Life You Dream

That which is meant for me readily comes to be.
Every day, in every way,
I allow myself to make whatever change my soul craves.
Even if I stand apart, I take the risks that heal my heart,
and I create the life I dream.

For Today

Write down one change you might like to make.

Notes

Overflow With Plenty

I place my bet on good.
I'm all in on happiness, on love gaining ground,
on blessings hanging around.
Peace takes a plate and feeds us from its bounty;
all who were hungry now overflow with plenty.
Hope reaches out until someone says *Yes*,
and we all surge forward in a stream of success.
All who were weary, whose minds sought a rest,
now are redeemed in love and kindness.

For Today

Allow your mind to rest.

Notes

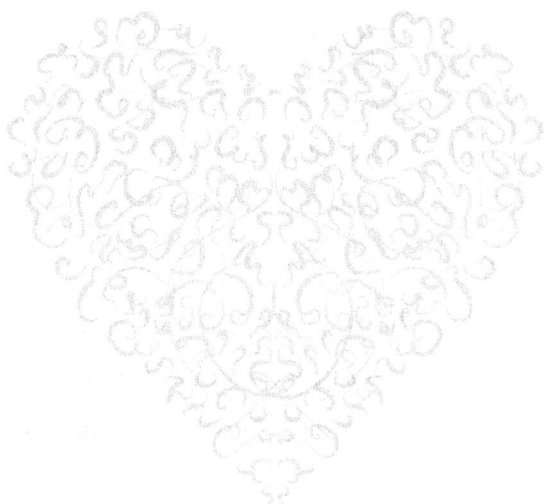

Anything Can Happen

In the midst of fear, I see a clearing—
a place where the world grows still.
Silence rests on a bird's wing.
Moments before the sparrow takes flight,
before ascension, before soaring.
The slightest breath begins to stir
with the chance that anything can happen.

For Today

Sense, if only for a second,
that moment before a bird takes flight.

Notes

Every Starburst Single Second

This day teaches me to see. I open my heart.

I open my mind.

There's no end to seeing, no end to what I find.

Who I am is in every breath,

in every starburst single second, in all the molecules,

fanned by the wind, and deeply connected to everything.

I am the luster, the halo.

I am the soul's call in the wind's howl,

the music underneath it all.

What lives in me lives forever,

what loves in me does not end.

For Today

The sacred is in every single second.

Notes

Ordinary Stardust

Today I look up when I'm down.

I remember the world is grand.

I see the stars that light the night

and know they're part of who I am.

Stardust and clay, earth composed in a human way,

I am ordinary stardust, wrapped in a mortal frame—

Love, light, and happiness with a human name.

Today I connect with all that is, with the light in every soul.

And as I do,

my inner self becomes more radiant and whole.

I am ordinary stardust, lit from within,

a mixture of happiness and love

ready to begin again.

For Today

Look up at the stars and know they are in you.

Notes

Reason And Rhyme

There is a solution. A reason. A rhyme.

There's an answer or two and it comes at the right time.

Today there are questions,

needs that are seen.

And now fall the answers like codes to a dream.

For Today

*Close your eyes and imagine answers to your questions
streaming down, finding you at just the right time.*

Notes

You Are Someone Special

This is you living your dream
so says the ocean as it roars to the shore,
so says the moonlight as it sparkles once more.
You are successful. You are someone special.
Keep going. Keep loving.
Keep being real.
The dream has a home inside your soul,
a place to thrive where it never grows old.
Keep going, keep loving,
keep living your life.
Doors once closed now open wide,
releasing a world filled with delight.

For Today

You are successful.
Who you are is someone special.

Notes

You Are The Flower Inside the Seed

I am the flower inside the seed,

searching for beauty, for what it can be.

I am the acorn that becomes the oak.

All that I see is in my own growth.

I am the flower, the tree, the moon and its beams.

I am in the light from above and the earth that I love.

All that is, is in my bones.

All that is, is my soul I behold.

All that is, is me coming home.

For Today

*Know that beauty is blooming within you
even when you feel like a dormant seed.*

Notes

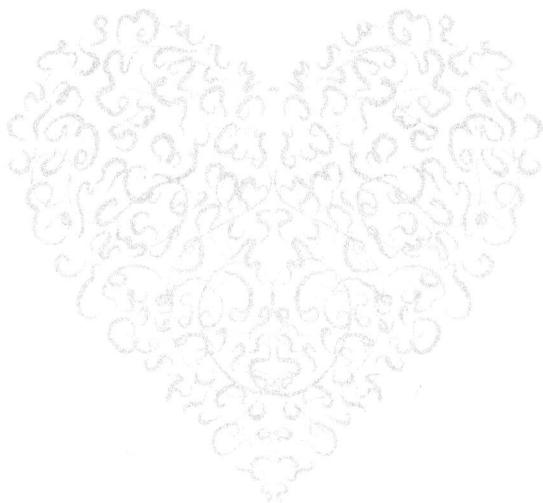

Within You
Is A Core of Gold

Within me is a core of gold, richer than the deepest mine.

Within me is a depth of soul,

more adventurous than any mountain I could climb.

The Source within me always was,

and will always be.

I am a flowering consciousness resonating as me.

For Today

You are golden, overflowing with light.
See it or just know it to be.

Notes

Waves Of Abundance

This enchanting day is filled with adventure
and new ways to play.
Waves of abundance flow my way.
Life is better than it's ever been,
sweet as a kiss you don't want to end.

For Today

Imagine the sweetness of a kiss.

Notes

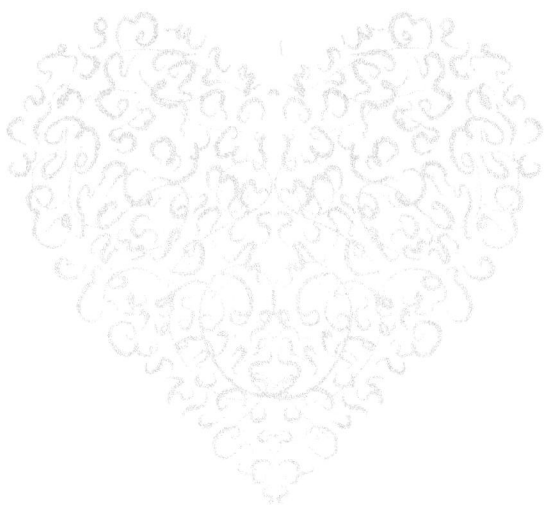

Riches Pour Forth

Doors once locked, now open wide.

Rewards once hidden are now magnified.

Riches pour forth in a passionate stream.

I am now everything I ever longed to be.

Each simple step leads to the next,

to more and more blessings,

graced from the Infinite.

For Today

You are graced with the wealth of the Infinite.

Notes

The Wild And Resilient Life Within You

The silver light that stirs the raucous sea

guides the wild and resilient life within me.

I learn to sail through rough waters and smooth,

finding my way even without light from the darkened moon.

Mine is the path of discovery.

I ride the currents like a fish in the sea,

the courage to navigate

somehow supplied to me.

Whatever the depths, I am submerged in trust.

The shimmering light that commands the infinite sea

now steers me perfectly.

For Today

Know that there is a wild and resilient life within you.

Notes

The Wonder Of Yes

I am the wonder of *yes*, the Infinite's love, divine success.

I am the dream. I am the goal.

I intuitively know which way to go.

Every next is met with success.

I am the wonder of Infinite Yes.

For Today

Know that you are the dream and the goal.
Your being is divine success.

Notes

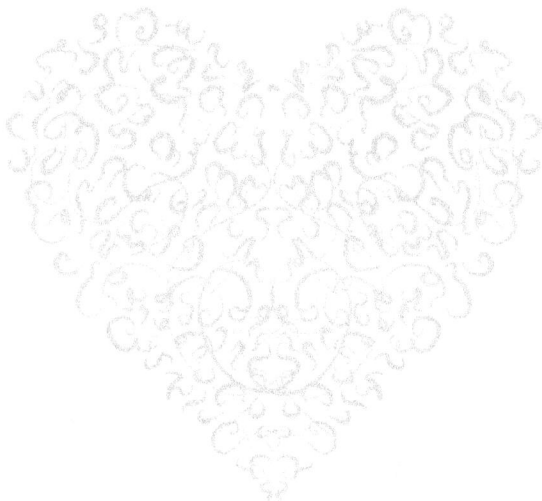

Pleasure Blooms From Everywhere

This day vibrates with the spirit of play,

a sense of joy that longs to stay.

Pleasure blooms from everywhere.

Listen…

the sound of children's laughter fills the air.

For Today

Imagine a sense of joy that longs to stay with you.
It shines down on you like the sun.

Notes

I Am The Light

I am the light I've been searching for,
the angel's breath that opens every door.
I am the love I've been hoping for,
the endless source that never needs more.
I am the light that is love that is like no other.

For Today

Be the light.

Notes

Inner Light

Even in the dead of night, the inner light maintains its glow.

A light so steady all will know,

this is who I am and why I'm here.

For Today

Let your inner light glow.

Notes

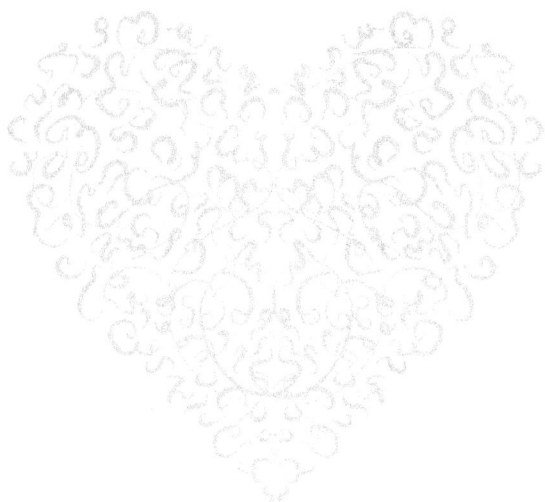

I Can See

Good fortune wraps me in its wings

and raises me above the clouds

where I can see everything—

the good, the bad, the in-between,

all that is and what strives to be.

Good fortune claims me for its own, its blessed child,

its cherished one.

I allow my heart and mind to rest.

For Today

You are the cherished one.
Allow your heart and mind to rest.

Notes

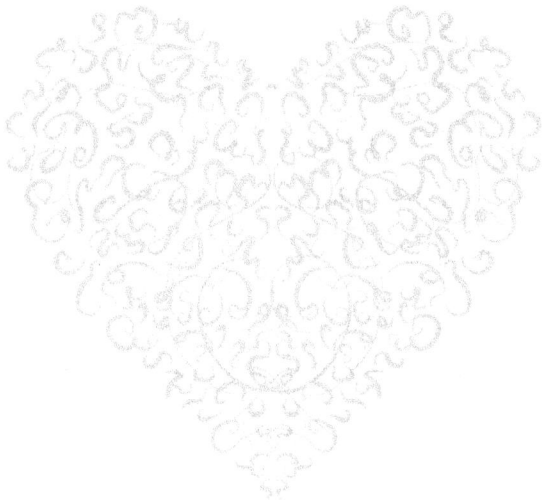

Drunk With Awe

From the mystic blue of a robin's egg
to the liquid light of the golden sun,
the rapture of this day melts my cares away.
As I drink in beauty,
I am drunk with awe.

For Today

Allow yourself to feel awe.

Notes

All That's Healing
Comes to Be

May all that's good and blessed and free,
may all that's perfect manifest for me.
May all that's healthy come to be.
May goodness grow and fear dissolve,
may every heart feel truly loved.
May all that's good and blessed and free,
all that's right come to be.
May every heart that seeks for more,
find it's true and just rewards.

For Today

Goodness grows and fear dissolves. Breathe that into your core.

Notes

Easily, Easily, Easily

I step into a world of miracles where all that can be can be.

My heart opens to my divine right fortune

and treasures come easily, easily, easily.

All that I need rests in my hands,

which reach to the sky and back again.

Blessings, like stars, illuminate the night,

lighting my life with well-being.

I am ready, I am willing,

I receive easily, easily, easily

all that is meant for me.

For Today

Imagine...you are stepping into a world of miracles.
Just follow the light, even if it's only a pinpoint.

Notes

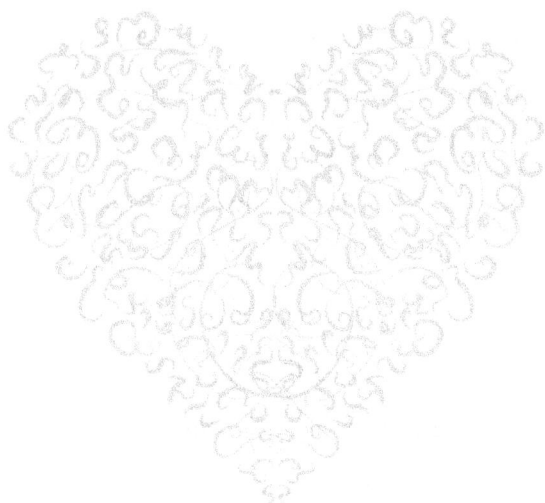

Only Good Can Come

The dappled sun through the willow trees
flickers its majestic warmth upon me.
I am blessed by the beauty of this day.
The prospering power that grew the canopy of willow trees,
and kissed me with its sacred breath,
now illuminates my every step with such intricacy
that I allow myself to trust.
It awakens the purest light within me.
And from this only good can come.

For Today

Imagine your path paved with luminous baby steps.

λ

Resources

None of us has to do it alone. Contact me at Lorrie@lorriekazan.com.

My website www.ilovemypsychic.com is regularly updated with helpful content. You can always suggest topics that relate to your particular interests or questions.

Sign up for my *One-Minute Meditations* and/or *Psychic Newsletter*. (It's the monthly for people who have no sense of time, meaning it was supposed to be monthly but it comes out a few times a year).

Come explore some of the services I offer. Sign up for a 15-minute psychic reading, or a half hour or more. Learn about who you are and what you came to this planet for.

Though the Edgar Cayce Institute (The Association for Research and Enlightenment) has chosen me as one of their top psychics, I still encourage every client to take the first five minutes of their reading and make sure they like my style. If not, we can stop, and I simply void the charge. Otherwise, we go on to create breakthroughs.

I read primarily by phone for people all over the world. I'm a bit like a plumber in people's lives, clearing out a lot of what's stuck or unseen. Telepathy, shapeshifting, healing, clairaudience, clairvoyance, and clairsentience are just some of the skills I practice.

What kinds of questions do people ask? Here are a few examples:

> My daughter won't return my phone calls. What's she thinking?
>
> My grandson (son, nephew, boyfriend…) is holed up in his room. Is he on drugs?
>
> What are his (or her) true feelings for me?
>
> Will this person call?
>
> What's my purpose in life?
>
> Will I have children?

My job is to connect with the higher world and make the unknown known. Sometimes that looks like a revelation of information and prediction. Other times it's more a mix of instructions for symbolic actions that, if taken, ultimately (or more immediately) open the path of greatest expansion.

What do you need to know?

Acknowledgements

Thank you to Dr. Aline LaPierre, who wrote the Foreword and believed in me well before I believed in myself; Dr. Henry Reed, from the Association for Research and Enlightenment, an early loyal supporter. The Association for Research and Enlightenment, an organization that transforms lives. And Edgar Cayce for offering a road map of what it means to be a psychic with integrity and humility.

Thank you to Diane Goldner, Chellie Campbell, Averi Torres; Laura Alden-Kamm, Elaine Wilson, Richard Brassaw, Louise Hawes, Victor Osaka, Christy Tryhus, Naomi Janzen, Peter Shea, Nancy Fursetzer, and Ann Maynard. Each person contributed in a unique and important way.

And thank you to the many wonderful clients, friends and family who have graced my life over the years. Thank you to those voices from the ethers that continue to light the path.

Index

www.ingramcontent.com/pod-product-compliance
Lightning Source LLC
Chambersburg PA
CBHW051824090426
42736CB00011B/1635